table of contents

"

Intimacy begins with oneself.
It does no good to try to find intimacy with friends, lovers, and family if you are starting out from alienation and division within yourself.

- Thomas Moore

"

introduction

It is 2012 and I'm standing in front of my dorm room mirror…on the verge of tears.

I'm the thinnest I've ever been and yet, I see a stretchmark forming on my body.
I audibly gasp, 'what is happening?!'. I'm in the gym every day, I'm barely eating, and I don't drink anything other than water, coffee & peppermint tea and *this* is what I get?

I stare into the mirror, hopeless – *my body is failing me*, I think.

I sit on my sink and take a picture to send to my mom and sister, needing to vent about the current, tragic blow to my ego. They assure me that it's nothing and tell me that I look great and 'really thin'. I thank them, but as I look at the picture, I hardly recognize myself.

In truth, I'm fucking miserable.

When you don't feel well on the inside, it's hard to believe you look well on the outside.
All I saw were the bags under my eyes, my underfed frame and my new archnemesis, the stretchmark.

At 18 years old, I have chronic migraines, early signs of clinical depression and zero social life…the stretchmark was the proverbial icing on the cake.

The nightly 'mirror meeting' I have with myself usually goes like this: I begin dissecting my appearance under fluorescent lighting and wonder why I listened to everyone about 'needing' to go to college. I wonder if everyone else is having a 'bad freshman year'. I then tell myself some bullshit story about how strong I am and how if everyone else can do it, so can I and I quickly get in bed, so I don't have to think anymore.

Tonight's mirror meeting goes differently though, I stare into my own eyes and my thoughts quickly shift to the bigger picture, *what am I doing here and when did my life get so sad?*

I grew up aiming to please; I wanted to be the perfect daughter & sister, I was obsessed with maintaining a 'good' reputation & I very rarely said, 'no'.
To be honest, my go-along-to-get-along attitude served me well during my primary years.
I was well-liked, trusted and known as a high energy extrovert yet, responsible.

I had it all figured out …or so I thought.

After high school graduation, I left the 'perfect' bubble I had created for myself and ventured off to college, in a city I had visited only once before.
After about a month of being settled into my single dorm room, I realized that I had no real direction, a stretchmark, and no idea who I was.
Once I was forced to sit alone with my own thoughts, a lot of things came up; emotions I thought I had suppressed, beliefs that I didn't even know existed and most importantly, unanswered questions that made me want to dive deeper.

I'd always thought of who I wanted to be, but I'd never really thought about who I actually was. I squint at my reflection, "who do you think you are?".

No, really…who do you *think* you are?
I don't mean, how do you think you appear to the outside world.
I mean, who are you when you strip away your current external realities?
Who are you without parental conditioning? When you silence the noise? When you look inward for validation rather than outward?
Who are you when you make choices solely based off your happiness and not the happiness of others? Without societal pressures and standards?
Who are you when you don't have migraines? When you love your body and nourish your mind?
Who are you when you embrace the stretchmark simply because it is a part of you?

Who do you think you are?

I needed to get to know myself – not who everyone else was comfortable with me being - I needed to get to know who I was without the influence, thoughts & projections of others.

When I took inventory of my life, I started to see patterns emerge regarding my relationships. Most of the friends I had at the time were miserable in their own lives and always complaining, I was stuck in a toxic romantic loop and my relationship with my family felt tense & unemotional. In short, I was surrounded by negative talk, accepting disrespect, feeling misunderstood and resentful of the fact that I wasn't living in my truth.

Then I started to see patterns emerge regarding my decision making. I had attended college because that's what everyone said I had to do. I went to the gym obsessively because I believed I had to maintain a certain weight in order to be attractive. I went to church every Sunday because that meant I was 'good' and would be rewarded. Realistically, I never wanted to go to college, I hated the gym and I didn't really believe in traditional concepts of religion.

Looking back, it is clear that my soul needed to be heard, but my ego resisted. If I dropped out of college, would people think I was stupid, unmotivated, or worse, would they think I was a failure? If I stopped dieting and going to the gym or had a stretchmark would people think I was lazy and had let myself go? If I started meditating instead of praying would my parents be disappointed?

Notice how everything I was questioning had to do with other people and their reactions to me.

Relying on external pleasures, attention, praise & validation was simply putting a band aid on a much larger issue. I was empty, confused and constantly trying to fill a gaping void that I couldn't find the root of. I wanted to move forward for myself, but I didn't know how.
What I did know was that I didn't want to live my life feeling like shit.

I didn't know it then, but the discovery of a tiny red mark on my skin was the beginning of my surrender. It was the first time ever that I couldn't hide an imperfection; I could stop myself from crying in front of people, I could put a fake smile on, I could bury myself in work to avoid dealing with reality, but I couldn't do anything about a stretchmark and honestly, something about that was liberating.

Being imperfect – physically, mentally & emotionally - felt like the real me.

I needed to get to know more of myself, even if it was uncomfortable and sometimes painful. I needed to discover what I liked and didn't like, to understand which were thoughts I was taught to think, and which were independent.

I *needed* to peel back the layers because I *wanted* to live better.

I wanted to know freedom, experience untouched intuition, listen to my gut and not question it. I wanted to make my own decisions simply because they made me happy, have healthy relationships and be able to communicate concisely & effectively. I wanted to be intentional and purposeful.

I wanted to trust myself, love myself and most importantly…I wanted to *like* myself, imperfections and all.

I realized that I couldn't satisfy any of those wants or needs until I knew my core. But, how was I going to get there? I felt stuck, but I knew that the more that I let the outside world dictate, the more miserable I was. The less I honored my truth, the less connected I felt to myself and what I knew was possible for my future.

So, I experimented.

I allowed myself to be led by my inner voice, not the external voices of others. I didn't know where the voice came from, I just knew that when I got really quiet, I could hear it. When I sat with myself & asked my own questions, I realized that I had the answers all along. A meek, inner voice told me to break up with my boyfriend because I deserved better. It told me to break up with some of my 'friends' as well - the constant complaints were weighing me down. Then, the voice got a little bit louder and told me not to return to campus in the fall and instead, move to New York City. It told me to start consuming more positive content, meditating, and reading self- help books. The voice told me not to be ashamed of asking for help. The more I paid attention to the whispers of my true self, the louder the voice got.
I realized; it was my soul talking.

My soul told me to do it afraid; it told me that these changes wouldn't be easy, but that they were necessary and would be worth it. It told me that small steps would eventually lead to big leaps and to trust myself. Most importantly, my soul told me that people weren't going to understand the moves I was about to make and that that was okay.

It was okay to be misunderstood by people who hadn't been where I wanted to go. It was okay to make decisions for me and not for others.

My soul told me that life is not about collecting compliments and constantly seeking approval, it's about being confident enough to be your true, authentic self & being willing to be misunderstood because of it.

So, I moved to New York at 19 years old, into an apartment by myself, boyfriend-less, with a small circle of long-distance friends, a couple of stretchmarks and without a fucking clue. I still had no idea what I was doing, but this time was different; I knew that if I listened to my soul, I would always find a way.

I was right.

Every difficult decision that I have made over the last nine years has paid off in full. I've learned tough lessons, cultivated amazing relationships, built businesses, and have really *lived*.
It hasn't ever been easy, but it has always been right for me.

My first 18 years of life were all about being a 'good' sister, daughter, student, employee, girlfriend, citizen, friend, etc. that I forgot to be a 'good' Devyn.
I wanted to write this guide because I believe most of us have forgotten to be a 'good'
(insert your name here).
We are so busy trying to be 'good' for everyone else that we neglect our true selves. What we don't realize is that when we know ourselves better, when we honor our soul desires & when we stop paying attention to what other people think of us, we become the person that we want to be. Scratch that…we become the person that we are *meant* to be.

We become purpose-driven and aligned, rather than money hungry and hustling.
We become confident and clear about what we want, rather than self-doubting and unsure.
We become loving and joyful, rather than judgmental and ungrateful.
We become the light that we have been seeking.
We realize that everything we need is within us.
Getting to know yourself is a process that requires patience, strength and a willingness to surrender. You must be ready to *feel* everything.
You'll laugh at yourself, you'll cry with yourself, you'll feel hopeless at times and on top of the world moments later. This guide is meant to help you work through those difficult moments of coming to terms with the fact that you've been living from the outside, in.
More importantly, it is meant to help you confidently begin living the amazing life that *is* yours.

My journey up until this point has been full of ups and downs.
I have failed many times, I've been in love many times, I've cried myself to sleep many nights and I've been the shoulder to cry on.

I have found success, I have been broke, I have made friends in the most unexpected places and I have seen some great ones go. I have beat myself up for having too much tequila, I've given myself endless pep talks, I've cursed my body for gaining weight and I've stood in the mirror checking myself out.

The beauty of living from the inside out is that you appreciate all moments equally. External circumstances are forever changing and so are feelings, but if you are tapped into your soul, you are unshakeable.

It is not about being perfect, in fact, it is about being imperfect and still knowing that you are fucking awesome. It is following your intuition, enhancing your relationships, and never settling. It is knowing your worth, speaking your truth and never feeling guilt, regret, or resentment again. It is about finding your metaphorical stretchmarks, staring at them, and loving them, simply because they are a part of you.

Being internally intimate is giving yourself permission to live fully.

You *are* the warrior, the truth-teller, the badass, the empath, the soul-searcher, the peacekeeper, the disruptor, the rockstar, the creator, the lover, the intuitive, the rebel, the eternal optimist.

You are so much more than who you have been told you are 'supposed to be'. It's time to de-program, re-program and return to yourself.

You aren't meant to live in a box that others have built for you.

You are simply and complexly meant to be *you*.

a note from devyn

I am not a clinical psychologist, nor am I a therapist or doctor. I am a life coach who specializes in intimacy; intimacy with self and intimacy with others. I draw from my own experiences and am simply a guide to those who are willing to become more connected to themselves in order to be more connected to the world around us.

My mission is, and has always been, to increase the amount of love in the world by showing people how to love themselves. Our souls know no hate, no injustice, no intolerance. Our community is global thus, our love knows no bounds.

However, we can only access that love when we are right with ourselves; mentally healthy, centered and at peace.

The reason I became a life coach is because I see the impact that soul-driven, empowered, loving humans can make in the world.

It is time to focus on love and it starts with us; it starts with us getting in touch with our soul, our inner calm and healing our hearts.
I am here to help guide the broken, the confused, the 'stuck', the tired, the overwhelmed, the saddened and the angry to a place of peace.
I am here to walk with you on your journey as you return to yourself.
People are my priority and we are ALWAYS better together.

PLEASE NOTE:
All exercises should be kept accessible throughout the 10-day process, as many of the exercises refer to the previous and build upon each other.

Please also advise that if at any time this process feels overwhelming or unmanageable to take a step back and finish the guide over a longer period of time.

Lastly, I love you and I'm here for you, always…I really mean that!

never hesitate to reach out & connect:
email: devyn@devynpenney.com

for more information or to book a one-on-one session, visit:
www.devynpenney.com

"

Knowing yourself
is the
beginning of all
wisdom.

- Aristotle

"

day 1 : ego vs. soul

EGO VS. SOUL

Let's take it back to the day you were born; you arrived a pure, free soul. Within moments of being birthed, you were then given a name, a gender, a race, a nationality, a religion (or lack thereof), a genetic code, etc. and just like that, your once pure, free soul becomes confined.
You immediately begin to develop a sense of attachment to the person, or people, who you perceive as your caretaker(s). That's right, our first understanding of emotion as human beings is not love, not hatred, not fear, not happiness, but *attachment*.
By the time you are eight months old, you will begin to feel anger and love, and by a year old you will be able to sense emotions of the people around you.
You spend the rest of your life honoring your attachments by trying to make sense of the identity you've been given. You do this by experimenting with behaviors, testing boundaries, and seeing how those around you emotionally react to you.
This is how you begin to form a sense of what is 'right' or 'wrong' and 'good' or 'bad'.
As our ability to understand the universal reward system develops, we realize that we want to be on the 'right' & 'good' side of things because that means that we will please the people we are most attached to.

Pretty interesting to think about it that way, isn't it?
Simply put, most of us live subconsciously honoring our attachments, not our souls. Let me be clear: this is no one's *fault*, this is a behavioral loop that has been played over infinite generations – we simply don't know any different. We are taught that if we abide by certain *rules*, that we are *good* and thus, will be rewarded. That said, we live our entire lives seeking reward by other people's standards based on their thoughts, beliefs, and conditioning.

Here's what we know for sure: your soul is lit.

Here's what we also know, once you've formed attachments to the outside world, it's hard for your soul to shine in the way it is meant to.
As we grow into our physical beings, we harden our outer shell in order to survive. The world we live in is oftentimes cold, negative, and hurtful, so we adapt.
As an infant, we can react, but we cannot control – thus, our ego begins to develop in order to gain a sense of control over external stimuli. This process continues over time; our ego is meant to help us gain perceived control over external circumstances…the key word being *perceived*, as all we can truly control is our emotional response.
By the time we are in our primary years, the superego begins to develop which incorporates our parental and societal conditioning.
Bottom line: we are led by the desire to control, fear of external circumstances and programming - rather than faith, love & truth.

The danger in allowing our ego to rule is that we risk the opportunity to fulfil our true potential. We cannot reach our highest self when acting from solely ego.

When in ego, we seek normalcy; we stay under the radar in fear of exposing imperfection, we try not to "rock the boat", we strive to be well-liked, we "play small" to avoid risk. We do these things, not because it is in our nature, but because we are told that this is the only way to exist in our world.

In reality, our souls want us to "play big", make noise, honor our desires, and get our needs met. Our souls want us to stop simply existing. Our soul wants us to *live*.

Your soul doesn't care about being well-liked by others, your soul cares about being well-liked by you. It is your ultimate guide and will take you to heights unknown to your physical self alone.

When you are in your soul, you will know only purpose, meaning & connectivity. When you are in your ego, you will know only greed, insecurity & competition.
Your soul is the observer of the ego; your ego is the destroyer of your soul.

EGO	SOUL
self-serving	altruistic
competitive	collaborative
seeks recognition	seeks authenticity
looks outward	looks inward
lusting	loving
attached to outcome	enjoys the process
causes pain	causes healing
feels lack	feels abundant
"should"	highest good
forced	flowing
limiting	empowering
greedy	generous
entitled	grateful
insecure	confident
complex	simplistic
prejudice	tolerant
distracted	present
mortal	everlasting

DAY 1 EXERCISE : GET STILL

Day 1 is about beginning to peel back the layers of ego in order to reveal your true, authentic self. The following exercise is meant to help you visualize your future self, clearly see your potential and realize what lies on the other side of living from your soul level.

It is important for you to hold this vision of your highest self close throughout this process in order to know what you are working towards (especially if/when difficult moments arise). Your highest self is who you are when you strip away your conditioning and eliminate the external noise. Your highest self is you; basking in the brightest light, living authentically, breathing deeply and knowing that you are exactly where you are supposed to be.

HIGHEST SELF (SOUL) MEETING MEDITATION & MANIFESTATION (20-25 MINUTES)

Silence and visualization are two of the greatest tools you have when getting to know yourself. Sitting still with your own thoughts allows your subconscious to reveal itself and visualization allows your soul desires to surface.

SILENCE /MEDITATION

For many people, meditation is intimidating, which is understandable because sitting with your own thoughts can be intimidating – you're never sure what's going to come up.
That said, you cannot let go of what you do not realize you're holding onto.
The key is to shift your perspective from being afraid of being alone with yourself to being grateful for the opportunity to work through thoughts and feelings that have been weighing you down.
The more you allow yourself to feel, the easier it is to let go of the negativity and make way for your highest self to show up.

VISUALIZATION /MANIFESTATION

Manifestation is the light amidst the darkness. The cool thing about your mind is that it won't allow you to visualize anything that isn't possible or attainable. Every daydream and vision that you have regarding your perfect life exists in real time and is waiting for you to claim what is yours. Having a clear vision of your future is what keeps you going during even the most difficult times. Knowing who you are capable of existing as and being able to see your own potential is one of life's greatest gifts.
Combining these two practices is extremely powerful and is the perfect way to begin your journey.

GUIDED MEDITATION : WWW.DEVYNPENNEY.COM/HIGHESTSELF

I've created this custom guided meditation in order to help you 'meet' your highest self.

The following recording is meant to be consumed while sitting or laying down in a comfortable, quiet place and will take approximately 15 minutes to run through (you can do it!).
Immediately following your meditation experience, please take another 5-10 minutes to record details of your highest self as you saw him/her in your meditation, be as specific as possible.
use the space provided below or a separate piece of paper that you can keep handy for the next 10 days

. . .

POST-MEDITATION JOURNALING

my highest self looks (get specific; hair color, what are you wearing?, etc.):

my highest self feels like:

my highest self lives (provide details of what you saw in your surrounding location):

my highest self does (for work/career/purpose):

my highest self does (for hobby/passion/lifestyle):

my highest self is with (who/what were you surrounded by):

other notes about your experience:

DAY 1 EXERCISE : EXAMPLE

POST-MEDITATION JOURNALING

my highest self looks

smiling, strong, fit, glowing, relaxed...

my highest self feels:

at peace, like I have purpose, happy with my decision making

my highest self lives (provide details of what you saw in your surrounding location):

in a warm climate, surrounded by palm trees and greenery

my highest self does (for work/career/purpose):

I own my own health food store

my highest self does (for hobby/passion/lifestyle):

I am active and do lots of yoga, hiking & cooking

my highest self is with (who/what were you surrounded by):

I'm not sure exactly who I was with, but I felt loved by them

other notes about your experience:

I felt really comfortable with myself and relaxed, almost relieved that everything had worked out. It was amazing to see myself having my dream life.

CONGRATULATIONS ON COMPLETING DAY ONE!

I hope that you enjoyed your Day 1 exercise and that you are going into the rest of your day/evening feeling a newfound sense of purpose and centeredness.
Please revisit this meditation as often as you'd like, especially when you need a reminder of who you are at your soul level.

You've gotten one step closer *to Mastering the Art of Internal Intimacy.*

I'm proud of you and you should be proud of yourself - see you tomorrow!
Ps. don't forget about the Day 1 journal page in the back of the workbook to write any additional thoughts, feelings or emotional responses that come up.

"

Energy comes from those you choose to surround yourself with.

Choose wisely.

- Karen Putz

"

day 2: influence by you

DIRECT INFLUENCES

Now that you've gotten a glimpse of who you are when you are living as your highest self and honoring your truth, it's time to talk about how to get there.

The first step is recognizing your conditioning so that you can begin to de-program.

We don't consciously realize it, but from the moment we are born, we are subconsciously conditioned by the people around us. In our youth, we are observers; we watch, we listen, we discover, and we dissect.

In our adulthood, we imitate.

On the most micro level, we are taught how to speak – take accents for example, they are passed down, not genetic. We find ourselves having aversions to things that our parents or caretakers disliked throughout our childhood. We develop nostalgia for traditions passed down and take comfort in daily routines that are created for us.

On a more macro level, we subconsciously adopt belief systems, morals and codes of conduct. We see the world through an extremely specific, carefully curated and narrowly-developed lens.

Our formative years are shaped by people telling us what is available to us or what is possible based on their experiences and we rarely question whether any of what we are being 'taught' is true for us.

We are constantly asked, "what we want to be", yet we rarely get asked *who* we want to be, or who we think we *are*, or what we *believe* in and we aren't told that there are multiple ways of thinking, doing and being.

That's right, there are multiple ways of existing. In fact, there are 7.8 billion (ish) ways to be a human. Revolutionary!

It's important to note that our conditioning is subconscious. Your direct influences don't usually realize that they are contributing to your deep, subliminal way of living. As said on Day 1, this is a generational loop that plays out over time and is fueled by 'societal norms' – you are deciding to break the chain.

You can't control influence, but you can manage it. As an adult, it is your job to examine your belief system, thought processes, customs, traditions, morals, etc. and decide which are serving you and which are weighing you down.

Getting clear about what you want vs. what your direct influences want for you is crucial in getting to know yourself on a soul level.

Here's the great news about de-programming old belief systems; you are 100% in control. You get to decide who you want to be and what your new belief system looks like. Sometimes this can feel overwhelming because there are so many possibilities, but really, it is exciting because there are so many possibilities!

You get to write this next chapter of your life as a freethinker. You get to decide what works for you and what doesn't. You get to decide what you would, could & should do next. You get to decide how to move through this world as your true, authentic self.

It's time to ask yourself the questions you wish you were asked as a child.

Who do you want to be? What do you believe in? What do you want to get out of your time here on earth?

If there are billions of options, how do you want to live?

DAY 2 EXERCISE: WRITING YOUR NEW CODE

We're going to write your new *code*; this is the metaphorical structure of your being. Your code is written over time and is made up of your beliefs, experiences, thoughts and influences.

Your current code reflects your current belief system, your new code determines what is actually true for you as you create your new belief system.

Just like a specific code ensures that all parts of a computer can communicate with each other, your human design code ensures that all parts of you are aligned and that your mind, body & soul are working together.

The great news is your code evolves as you do and can be written and re-written as many times as you'd like to make an 'edit' to your internal system.

De-programming old beliefs can be challenging because we usually don't realize that we have been programmed in the first place. This exercise is meant to help you identify how your current code is written and then, editing it to reach full mind-body-soul alignment. It's time.

THE (ANTI) BLAME GAME

While completing this exercise, it is imperative that you keep an open, honest mind and that you stay as objective as possible. You may find yourself blaming others for the influence (negative or positive) that they've had on you and that is completely counterproductive.

It is important to note two things:

1. Everyone does the best they can with the tools that have at any given moment. Everyone in our lives has been programmed from birth as well; the beliefs that they pass down to you are simply the result of their own programming. You are deciding to break generational chains, which is amazing, but it is also your journey and yours alone.

2. If you are going to blame people in your life for the 'bad', you must also blame them for the 'good'.

HONESTY HOUR

I've said it before, and I will say it again; this process can be uncomfortable at times. You are doing amazing, but hard work. Part of getting to know yourself is about getting honest with yourself and while this exercise will help you better understand your current belief system, it might also bring up some feelings that are new or that have been suppressed. Stay honest and take a step back when you need to – this is a marathon, not a sprint.

You've probably heard it before: you are a product of the people you surround yourself with. The people you speak to most often, spend the most time with, look up to, etc. are the people you are most directly influenced by. These are the attachments; the people you feel an underlying loyalty to, the ones you are aiming to please, whether consciously or subconsciously.

Your words, actions, beliefs and thoughts are a result of their words, actions, beliefs and thoughts. It's not that these characteristics are *wrong* or *problematic*, many of them are just not *yours*. Let's see which traits you want to bring with you on the journey to your highest self and which no longer serve you.

use the space provided or a separate piece of paper that you can keep on hand for the next 9 days

STEP ONE

In the circles on the next page, write the names of 2 people you believe are the most direct influences in your life (think parents, caretakers, best friends, mentors, etc.). In the circle under their names, write their positive traits/characteristics on the right and their negative traits/characteristics on the left.

This is not about judging your loved ones or community; this is about understanding where your programming comes from and deciding which traits you'd like to continue to possess and which you'd like to cancel.

STEP TWO

Now in the middle of the two circles, write the characteristics and beliefs that you identify with from that person – both negative and positive. This requires you to take a step back and be objective; again, it is not about judging yourself, it is about having awareness.

STEP THREE

Take the positive traits, characteristics beliefs that you identify with that you would like to maintain.
In the space provided, write, "I am/I have_____".
Your new code is who you *are*.

STEP FOUR

Now take the characteristics and beliefs that you have inherited that you would like to cancel.
In the space provided, write "I cancel _____".
When you begin to feel your negative program taking over, cancel it and replace it with your new code.

NAME OF INFLUENCE #1

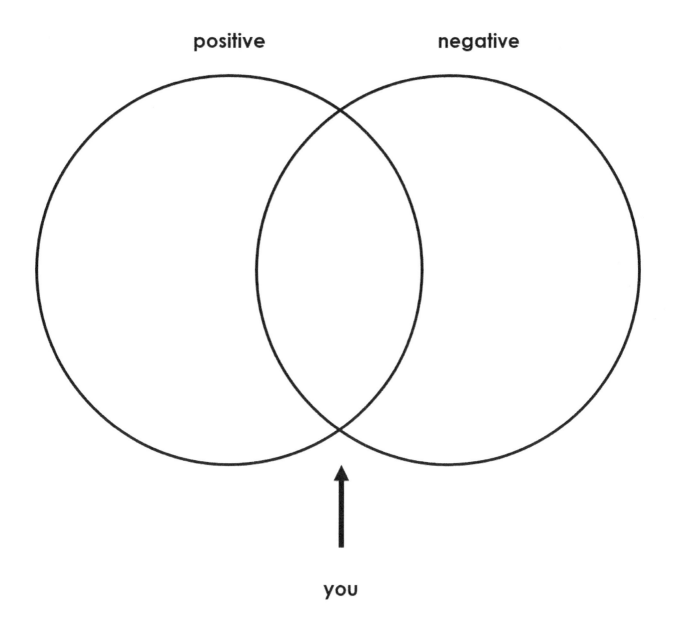

positive   negative

you

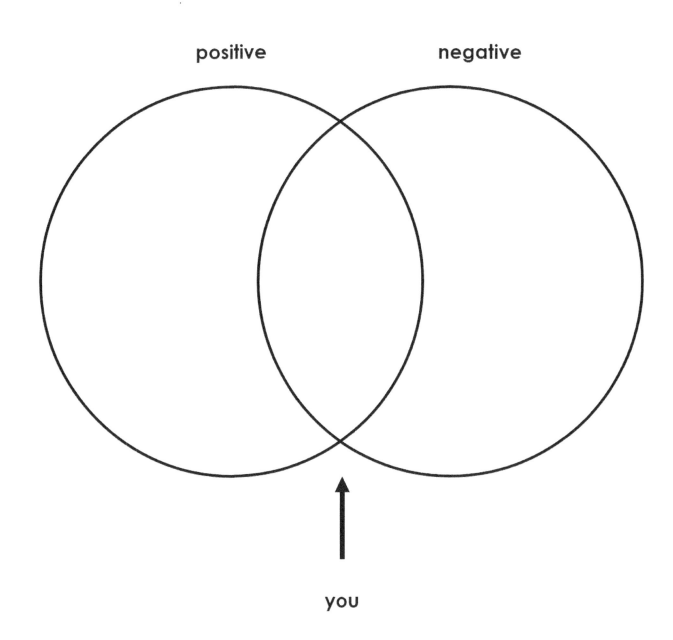

YOUR OLD CODE

I consciously decide to rewrite my programming;
I no longer allow negative programming to hinder me from reaching
my fullest potential in life.
I cancel what no longer serves me, my old code is behind me.

I CANCEL...

YOUR NEW CODE

I consciously decide to rewrite my programming;
I no longer allow negative programming to hinder me from reaching
my fullest potential in life.
I cancel what no longer serves me, my new code is who I am.

I AM/I HAVE...

DAY 2 EXERCISE : EXAMPLE

mother
_____

NAME OF INFLUENCE #1

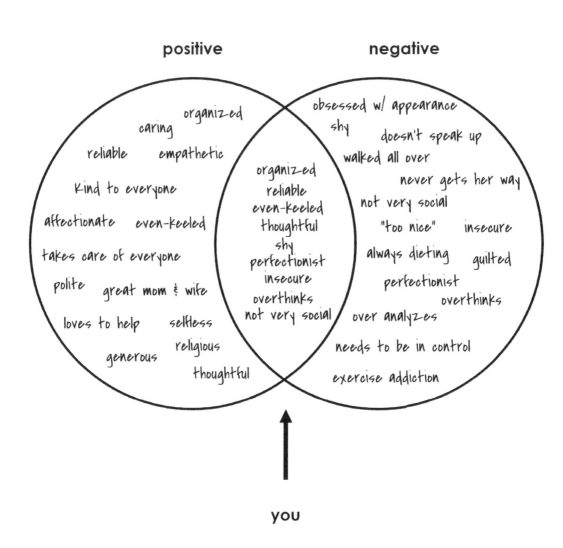

positive   negative

organized
caring
reliable   empathetic
kind to everyone
affectionate   even-keeled
takes care of everyone
polite   great mom & wife
loves to help   selfless
generous   religious
thoughtful

organized
reliable
even-keeled
thoughtful
shy
perfectionist
insecure
overthinks
not very social

obsessed w/ appearance
shy
doesn't speak up
walked all over
never gets her way
not very social
"too nice"   insecure
always dieting   guilted
perfectionist
overthinks
over analyzes
needs to be in control
exercise addiction

you

YOUR OLD CODE

I consciously decide to rewrite my programming;
I no longer allow negative programming to hinder me from reaching
my fullest potential in life.
I cancel what no longer serves me, my old code is behind me.

I CANCEL...

being shy around people

the need for perfection

any & all insecurity regarding my personality and/or personality

overthinking

social anxiety

YOUR NEW CODE

I consciously decide to rewrite my programming;
I no longer allow negative programming to hinder me from reaching
my fullest potential in life.
I cancel what no longer serves me, my new code is who I am.

I AM/I HAVE...

reliable

organized in my personal & professional life

even-keeled/ even-tempered

thoughtful & considerate

CONGRATULATIONS ON COMPLETING DAY TWO

You came back, and you did it!
I'm so excited to continue on this journey with you and am especially excited that you are now one step closer to reaching soul-level consciousness.
Keep up the great work, see you tomorrow.
Ps. don't forget about the Day 2 journal page in the back of the workbook to write any additional thoughts, feelings or emotional responses that come up.

"

Conformity is the jailer
of freedom and the
enemy of growth.
- John F. Kennedy

"

day 3 : society by you

"THEY SAY"

Day 2 was all about recognizing the programming you receive from the people you are closest and most attached to. Day 3 is about understanding how said programming originated and how it gets passed down from generation-to-generation through society.

We've already established that no one is born with hatred, biases, jealousy, intolerance, insecurity, etc., so why is it that almost every human on the planet suffers from one or more of these negative concepts?

I call them, "concepts" because they are; success is a concept, modern-day religion is a concept, insecurity is a concept, beauty is a concept…the basis of our belief systems, self-esteem and world views are simply thoughts that have caught on and stuck.

Let's take it back to 2.5 million years ago:
- everyone had the same skin color
- there wasn't a trade system or currency
- people weren't walking around, worried about other people judging 'that extra five pounds'
- there weren't places of worship
- …and school wasn't even a thought

Of course, we have since evolved on every single level, but it would be remiss to not mention that the cultural, physical and societal standards that we currently abide by are man-made. If you really take a step back and think about that, it puts a lot of things into perspective; there is no superior race, religion or belief system. There is no actual standard of beauty. There is no real definition of success. In the same way that these ideas came about, they can be taken out by *you* - an equivalent human being who gets to write their own story and live by their own rules.

If you were to look up the definition of any of today's buzz words, they do not prioritize physical appearance, nor do they identify a superior trait, set of beliefs or aesthetic.

Take the word, "beauty" for example, the dictionary defines the noun as, "the quality present in a thing or person that gives intense pleasure or deep satisfaction to the mind, whether arising from sensory manifestations (as shape, color, sound, etc.), a meaningful design or pattern, or something else (as a personality in which high spiritual qualities are manifest)". Do you see, "tall, skinny with blonde hair and blue eyes" or "washboard abs, chiseled jawline and perfect hairline" anywhere in that definition? No. So how did those things become the modern-day 'physical standard'? People, just like you and me, have decided that those are the standards of beauty based on biases formed by 'superior' races and ethnicities over centuries. Yet, we sit around feeling like shit about ourselves because we aren't what society has told us is beautiful, or smart, or successful, or 'right' and 'just'.

We spend our entire lives trying to adjust to what *they* want, what *they* say, what *they* believe because we are made to think that what *they* want for us is more important than what *we* want for us. Then, we wonder why we end up totally miserable – hint hint: it's because we're living for other people.

A lot of people speak of freedom as independence from others – when really, freedom is the ability to live as our authentic selves.

Who you are at your soul-level is loving, free, empowered & purely joyful - there is no fear, no insecurity, no anxiety, etc.

We grow up around other humans who have been conditioned to be the versions of themselves that society deems acceptable. We are given a set of standards that we are dying (literally) to live up to, but that we never stop to question. We are told what is best for us; how we should look, how we should act, even what we should do with our lives…and then, we are told that not living up to said standards equals a failed existence.

This is a story that has been invented and reinvented by man for many centuries:

- The notion of 'good behavior' or modern-day etiquette originally began as a way to keep societal order and to teach ancient Egyptians how to best serve their masters.

- Today's conventional schooling exists because working children were required to learn lessons of, obedience, suppression of their own will and show loyalty towards masters.

- The undisputed 'regular' workday was put in place so that people could work longer hours in factories and the term 9-5 is often negatively used to describe a, 'tedious or unremarkable occupation'.

- Live Science notes that, "being overweight was considered beautiful and ideal until 1840 when a Presbyterian Minister began advocating a plain diet for women because, 'spices, stimulants and other overindulgences lead to indigestion, sexual excess & civil disorder'".

Are you seeing what I'm seeing? Themes of suppression, obeying masters, keeping order and control.

In some cultures, religions and time periods, it was said that a rebellious spirit could even result in death.

Here's a question for you: who is your master? Who is it that you are being obedient to? Are you suppressing your spirit to maintain order in your world?

Here's a bigger question for you: what would your life look like if your soul were your master? What would it feel like for you to listen to and obey your intrinsic needs? What would it be like to allow your spirit to rebel against what you have been told is right for you and to actually do what is right for you?

Damn.

While you've been looking to the external world to make sense of your life, you've had the answers internally, the whole time.

Are you getting where I'm going with this? It's time to take all of the bullshit that *they* made up, chuck it out the window and start over. It's time to unlearn what *they* have taught us and live from the inside out. It's time to consciously rebel.

DAY 3 EXERCISE: YOU VS. THEM

We've determined that many of your beliefs about how you 'should' be living, behaving and believing come from the metaphorical *them* (society), but what does it look like when *you* live, behave and believe what *you* know is right for *you*?

Something I hear from my clients is that they don't know what they want when society isn't telling them how to exist. My answer is always, of course you do! Your soul was dropped into your body knowing exactly what to do; your soul knows it's purpose, your soul knows what you need more or less of, you just have to listen.

This exercise is meant to make you take a step back and really think about who you are living for; is it for the acceptance, approval and validation of others? Or are you living for you?

STEP ONE

In the left-hand column, write the phrases, stereotypes, beliefs, etc. that you have heard throughout your life about what is 'acceptable' or that you 'should' be doing.

STEP TWO

In the right-hand column, write your soul-level beliefs in comparison.

This piece of paper is a no-judgement zone. you don't have to explain why you feel, believe or want the things that you do. You don't have to make excuses or defend yourself. You don't have to argue with people who feel differently. You just have to honor your truth. I will continue to say this: the programming we have received from society is not necessarily 'bad' or 'wrong', but it might not be yours. Start defining yourself by your thoughts, beliefs and truths, rather than by what *they* say.

THEY SAY	I SAY

DAY 3 EXERCISE : EXAMPLE

THEY SAY	I SAY
"you have to get married & have kids to feel fulfilled"	I do not need a person or children to fulfill me and am open to many versions of loving relationships.
"you're not good looking unless you look like a celebrity"	I'd rather feel good on the inside than obsess over my outward appearance.
"if you 'sin', you're going to hell"	I make decisions that are right for me and I know that higher power supports me.
"pick one: career or family"	I live my life using AND instead of OR
"having casual sex is inappropriate"	everyone's body is theirs and they make the decisions - I love feeling sexy and I have nothing to be ashamed of.
"going to college is the only way to succeed"	I'm grateful to live in a time where education on all levels is so accessible, I am curious & can figure anything out.
"if you make lots of money you will be happy"	there are so many ways to measure personal wealth & money isn't one of them. I am abundant in all ways, always.

CONGRATULATIONS ON COMPLETING DAY THREE

How do you feel? Whatever you're feeling right now is valid and necessary; some will feel an immediate release by doing these three days of exercises and others will feel overwhelmed or identity-less.

Neither response is better or worse, it is simply yours. Allow yourself to feel everything – you're unpacking years of conditioning in a short period of time, it's okay to feel the weight of that. Emotions are healthy as long as you don't let them get stuck inside of you – let them move through you and get excited for Day 4.

You're doing great and I'm really happy for you, you're changing your life…pretty amazing!

Ps. don't forget about the Day 3 journal page in the back of the workbook to write any additional thoughts, feelings or emotional responses that come up.

"

If you end up with a boring, miserable life because you listened to your mom, your dad, your priest, or some guy on tv telling you how to do your shit...you deserve it.

- Frank Zappa

"

day 4: inadequacy vs you

THE GUILT, THE SHAME & THE INSECURITY

We can't talk about direct influences and societal pressure without discussing guilt, shame and insecurity. Oftentimes, these three emotional experiences are biproducts of living from the outside in. We feel guilt if we don't honor our attachments, we feel shame when we don't live up to societal standards and we feel insecurity when we find ourselves pulled between our truth and the opinions of others.

Let's explore each of these experiences individually, I have built in the Day 4 exercises for you to complete along the way.

GUILT

If you have a conscious and you're not a psychopath (literally), chances are you've experienced guilt. This impending feeling of being wrong, doing wrong - or failing to do - contributes to the belief that we are not enough. Like every other emotional response, guilt is a result of our programming and conditioning. As children, we are told what is right or wrong, good or bad according to our influences and society and as adults, if/when we go against said conditioning, we feel an immediate sense of responsibility to right our perceived wrongs. While a healthy sense of guilt motivates us to be ethical, 99% of our guilt is created unnecessarily. In fact, according to the dictionary definition, guilt is, 'feeling responsible or regretful for a perceived offense, real or imaginary". Read that last line again.

Our brain cannot decipher between real and imaginary; it is our conditioning that elicits the same amount of guilt regardless of circumstance. For example, if you say something that hurts someone's feelings you may feel guilty, uncomfortable and even have anxiety over your actions. Most times, these feelings will eventually lead you to offer an apology and do what is necessary until the other person feels better and you feel clear. Now, if you're late to your mom's birthday party because you had to work late, you will experience the same amount of guilt, discomfort and anxiety. This is not because these emotions are warranted in this situation, this is because you've been conditioned to believe that you should place family above all else. When you prioritize work, even if it's necessary, guilt creeps up in a way that can be debilitating. As said, our brains cannot decipher where to place the proper amount of guilt…so you're going to have to tell it how.

GUILT EXERCISE

The goal of this exercise is not to rid yourself of the 'good' kind of guilt, it is to realize which imaginary offenses you allow to elicit a strong, unnecessary emotional response. Think about two things that you find yourself feeling constantly guilty about and fill in the blanks below.

GUILT

noun: blame; bad conscience over responsibility

I feel guilty when _____,

this makes me feel guilty because

_____.

So I end up _____,

When I really want to:

_____.

I feel guilty when _____,

this makes me feel guilty because

_____.

So I end up _____,

When I really want to:

_____.

GUILT

noun: blame; bad conscience over responsibility

I feel guilty when <u>I miss family events</u> ,

this makes me feel guilty because
<u>my family makes me feel like I am missing out & don't care</u> .

So I end up <u>rearranging my life to fly home for everything.</u> ,

When I really want to:
<u>facetime them & call it a day.</u> .

I feel guilty when <u>I say 'no' to plans with my friends</u> ,

this makes me feel guilty because
<u>I don't want them to think I don't like them or for them not to like me.</u>

So I end up <u>I agree to everything, even if it's inconvenient</u> ,

When I really want to:
<u>stay in, relax, recharge & save money.</u> .

~~GUILT~~ *FREEDOM*

noun: independent, license to do as one wants

Because I am _____,

I choose to

_____.

Doing this will _____,

and I know that

_____.

I feel guilty when _____,

this makes me feel guilty because

_____.

So I end up _____,

When I really want to:

_____.

~~GUILT~~ *FREEDOM*

noun: independence, license to do as one wants

Because I am <u>I am very busy living & working</u>,

I choose to
<u>pick 3 family events to attend this year</u>.

Doing this will <u>alleviate stress & let me plan ahead</u>,

and I know that
<u>my family will understand and love me no matter what</u>.

Because I am <u>someone who needs alone time</u>,

I choose to
<u>honor myself and stay in when my body/mind/bank account tell me to</u>.

Doing this will <u>give me the rest that i need to be a better friend</u>,

and I know that
<u>my friends will respect that & appreciate my reset</u>.

SHAME

Shame is one of our deepest, most overpowering emotions, yet is usually not spoken about or is passed off as guilt. If guilt is feeling bad about your behavior, shame is feeling bad about yourself. Guilt is what you did or did not *do*, shame is *who* you are and *who* you are not. As Brenè Brown would say, "Guilt is, 'sorry, I made a mistake.' Shame is, 'sorry, I *am* a mistake'". Again, shame is a direct result of our conditioning; if we are shamed as a child or see our direct influences or society shaming someone else, it sticks with us. Both guilt and shame trigger the same fear in us, however our responses to the two ends up being different. Unlike guilt, we oftentimes believe that our feelings of shame are so deep rooted that we cannot do anything to rectify them and subsequently turn to more destructive behaviors to cope and/or block out the feeling. Oftentimes, our shame leads us to worsen the situation because on some level, we believe that we're hopeless. For example, if you come from a very conservative family and are shamed for being 'different' due to your appearance, behavior or views, the natural emotional response is to rebel more extremely.

The problem with this is that your behavior becomes a direct response to external circumstances and what others think, want and expect from you. When we live in shame, we live in a world that doesn't belong to us; we're held captive by a strange comfort in shock value and disappointment. Why suffer and self-destruct for someone else's approval or satisfaction? The repercussions of this behavioral loop are damaging, long-lasting and completely ego driven. When you begin living from the inside out, you choose vulnerability and honesty over shame. You recognize your imperfections as marks of authenticity and uniqueness. You realize that being different is both subjective and usually a blessing. Most importantly, you live seeking the approval of only your soul.

SHAME EXERCISE

The goal of this exercise is to create a space where you can be honest about when you feel shame and how you directly respond to that feeling. Be objective, be vulnerable (these pages are for you) and take control of your life and your emotional response to the outside world. You are not a mistake, nor must you live in the constant state of shame that others have imposed on you.

Think about two things that you find yourself feeling constantly shameful about and fill in the blanks below.

SHAME

noun: disgrace, embarrassment

I feel shame when _____,

this makes me feel shameful because

_____.

So I end up _____,

When I really want to:

_____.

I feel shame when _____,

this makes me feel shameful because

_____.

So I end up _____,

When I really want to:

_____.

SHAME

noun: disgrace, embarrassment

I feel shame when <u>I have to explain that I'm not dating anyone,</u>

this makes me feel shameful because
<u>I am in my 30's and I should have a partner by now</u> .

So I end up <u>lying about my dating life</u> ,

When I really want to:
<u>tell them they should be asking me about my awesome career, not my</u>.
<u>relationship status.</u>

I feel shame when <u>someone asks me about money</u> ,

this makes me feel shameful because
<u>I have no savings & it makes me feel irresponsible</u> .

So I end up <u>talking about material things to impress them</u> ,

When I really want to:
<u>talk about the book I just read and loved</u> .

~~SHAME~~ *HONESTY*

adjective: truthful, candid

Because I am _____ ,

I choose to

_____ .

Doing this will _____ ,

and I know that

_____ .

Because I am _____ ,

I choose to

_____ .

Doing this will _____ ,

and I know that

_____ .

~~SHAME~~ *HONESTY*

adjective: truthful, candid

Because I am <u>an adult</u>,

I choose to
<u>not answer & tell people that I like to keep my private life private</u>.

Doing this will <u>put up a healthy boundary</u>,

and I know that
<u>I will then be able to redirect the conversation to my career</u>.

Because I am <u>not interested in money talk</u>,

I choose to
<u>lead (or re-direct) with conversations about other interests</u>.

Doing this will <u>let others know what my interests are</u>,

and I know that
<u>I will begin to attract more like-minded people to me</u>.

INSECURITY

From physical appearance and career anxiety, to imposter syndrome and an overwhelming sense of unworthiness, constant feelings of guilt and shame create a plethora of insecurities. Here's the thing about insecurities: they have nothing to do with you. ALL of your insecurities come from your environment and your conditioning. Need proof? Did you come out of the womb crying and think, *I hope all of these doctors aren't judging my naked body*!? No. You spent years watching your mother look in the mirror while she was getting ready to talk about those 'extra 5lbs' she wanted to lose. You spent years going to school with other kids who were conditioned by their direct influences and projected those insecurities onto you also. You spent years reading magazines, watching TV and scrolling through social media, only to see one body type represented. You spent years listening to the world tell you that you can only get rich by going to college and getting a 9-5 job…and by the way you must be rich, it's the only way to be happy. You spent years hearing about the glass ceiling, the white picket fence and the corporate ladder. You spent years trying to fit into this very tiny, very average box to make the world more comfortable with your place in it. When you started to bust out of the box, someone came and put more tape on the seams and plastic wrapped it.

Now, you've lost the 5lbs, gotten the plastic surgery, worked out every day, gone to college, gotten a 9-5, climbed the corporate ladder, touched the glass ceiling, built the white picket fence…and you're still miserable (and cramped) in this damn box.

Great news: your soul sent me here with a box cutter. It's time to break out, to escape the strong holds of your direct influences & society. It's time to stop listening to people who only see one way of doing things and who project what they believe to be possible for themselves onto you. It's time to stop following the crowd…they're lost as fuck.

INSECURE EXERCISE

We're going to talk more about your insecurities on Day 5, but this exercise will get you to begin turning your insecurities into empowered action. Ready? Let's do it.

INSECURE

adjective: uncertain, worried

I feel insecure when _____,

this makes me feel insecure because

_____.

So I end up _____,

When I really want to:

_____.

I feel insecure when _____,

this makes me feel insecure because

_____.

So I end up _____,

When I really want to:

_____.

INSECURE

adjective: uncertain, worried

I feel insecure when I look at Instagram & see perfect bodies ,

this makes me feel insecure because
I want to lose 20lbs and feel unattractive .

So I end up Feeling hopeless, beating myself up & comfort eating ,

When I really want to:
love my body & feel healthy and attractive .

I feel insecure when I talk about my career ,

this makes me feel insecure because
my job is not a traditional 9-5 .

So I end up downplaying myself & my work ,

When I really want to:
tell people about what I do and promote myself .

INSECURE   *EMPOWERED*

verb: to be in power, to give permission

Because I am _____,

I choose to

_____.

Doing this will _____,

and I know that

_____.

Because I am _____,

I choose to

_____.

Doing this will _____,

and I know that

_____.

DAY 4 EXERCISE : EXAMPLE

INSECURE   *EMPOWERED*

verb: to be in power, to give permission

Because I am smart, kind, thoughtful, generous & worthy ,

I choose to
love myself for exactly who I am .

Doing this will make me feel better about myself ,

and I know that
I am exactly where I need to be & can better my health at any time .

Because I am a badass creator ,

I choose to
have confidence in my work & sing my own praises in public .

Doing this will remind me of my power & bring in business ,

and I know that
others will begin to see what I see in myself .

CONGRATULATIONS ON COMPLETING DAY FOUR

I find Day 4 to be one of the most freeing and revealing days of the de-programming phase. In order to properly complete those exercises, you have to get extremely honest and vulnerable (the only known antidotes to guilt, shame and insecurity).

Today, I hope you feel powerful, knowing that you have options; you have the option to live a life of freedom and truth…and feel great about it.

You're killing this 10-day guide – keep it up!

Ps. don't forget about the Day 4 journal page in the back of the workbook to write any additional thoughts, feelings or emotional responses that come up.

"

When you do
shadow work,
you are doing
the work of radical
self acceptance.

- Unknown

day 5 : you by you

SHADOW WORK

We have analyzed our direct influences, begun to de-program from societal conditioning and have canceled toxic emotional responses and old beliefs. In previous days, we have explored how external people and circumstances impact you, now, it's time to take a look at what psychology calls *your shadow*. Your shadow is your dark side, your subconscious, your primitive self; it is the part of you that you don't want anyone to know about or see. Although we are taught to repress our shadow it never goes away. In fact, the less we pay attention to it the larger it gets, until our actions are simply a projection of our dark side. As 20th century psychologist Carl Jung said, "Everyone carries a shadow and the less it is embodied in the individual's conscious life, the blacker and denser it is".

The point of doing shadow work is to acknowledge and befriend your shadow, rather than continue to repress and hide it. Perhaps best explained by the ancient Chinese philosophy of yin and yang or 'duality', we need both light and darkness to make ourselves whole. Many people associate darkness with danger, sinful behavior or taboo, when really, darkness is simply a part of us. As a human will never not cast a shadow behind them in the light, our shadow remains attached to us no matter what. As adults, it is our job to explore our shadow until it no longer scares us. We cannot expect to live only in light, in fact, when the light is brightest, our shadow is the darkest. We must accept and rationalize both parts of ourselves until they coexist in harmony.

Doing this work is difficult; it is sometimes uncomfortable, but ultimately, it will give you a greater sense of self by bringing clarity and peace. Society tells us that our shadows are unacceptable; we are taught to conceal any parts of ourselves that are less than 'perfect' (according to the masses). The danger in allowing our shadow selves to overpower is that we begin to see our sadness, pain and resentment manifest into anger issues, addictions, self-loathing and even disease. Ignoring our shadow takes a physical and mental toll on us, as it is another example of us not allowing our truth to shine through. Jung points out, "one does not become enlightened by imagining figures of light, but by making the darkness conscious".

Our shadow is subconscious, which means that we might not be able to directly identify when it is at work, but our conscious reality is that most of what we perceive as injustice, pain, suffering and wrong-doing in the world is a direct mirror of our shadow. We oftentimes find ourselves being triggered by people who possess our same weaknesses or who possess a strength that we wish we possessed. For example, it is only a person who is outwardly loud who finds themselves annoyed by or uncomfortable with shy or quiet people – that is because *stillness or quiet* is a subconscious trait that they struggle with. The same is true for quieter people who find loud individuals to be annoying, overbearing and uncomfortable. The ability to speak up is a subconscious desire and thus, they are triggered by those who so freely do so. In this case, both people's annoyance and discomfort is a projection of their shadow.

The only way to ensure that our shadow is not subconsciously ruling our outward behavior is to confront it, understand it and appreciate it. It is always hard to face pain, repressed emotions and insecurities, but it is also necessary. By mastering your shadow, you relinquish your title as the victim and instead become even more powerful. As said before, we need a balance of light and dark in order to be a whole, balanced human. All parts of you are necessary and are meant to teach you and help you grow. By doing the introspective work that is *shadow work*, you will be able to relieve your subconscious and accept yourself and your soul, by honoring your truth.

Shadow work will oftentimes lead to waking up parts of ourselves that we didn't even know existed. Mastering your shadow leads to mass creativity, freedom of thought and a deeper understanding of purpose.

DAY 5 EXERCISE: MASTERING YOUR SHADOW

Your shadow consists of your insecurities, pain points, your self-doubt, your outdated beliefs and your toxic coping mechanisms.

As said above, the best way to make peace with your shadow is to confront it and that's what this exercise is all about. It is meant to make you face your shadow head on and allow your soul to heal it. Allow yourself to feel through this process; let your emotions flow through you – no one has ever healed without feeling. The point of this exercise is to see clearly the part of yourself that you try to hide from the world and to allow it to exist without succumbing fully to the darkness.

STEP 1

Go back to your Day 2 completed exercise, take 'I am'/ 'I have' statements from your 'new code' and write them around the yellow figure on the next page.

Go back to your Day 4 completed exercise, take the things that make you feel free, empowered & honest and write them around the shadow figure as well.

This is your soul speaking.

STEP 2

Go back to your Day 2 completed exercise, take the words/phrases from your 'old code' that you have decided to cancel and write them around the shadow figure.

Go back to your Day 4 completed exercise, take the things you feel guilty, shameful and insecure about and write them around the shadow figure as well.

Add any other negative thoughts, behaviors, coping mechanisms or thoughts around the shadow figure.

STEP 3

On the next page, write what you want to say to your shadow, from your soul. Tell your shadow that you acknowledge it, that you know it is a part of you and that you choose to lead with your soul, your truth and your light. When your soul is in charge, you are powerful.

YOU

SOUL in charge
(shadow is small)

DAY 5 EXERCISE : EXAMPLE

thoughtful   even keeled

considerate   empathetic

kind   YOU   reliable

enjoying life   generous

confident   patient

decisive   badass

↑

creator   **SOUL** in charge
                                 (shadow is small)

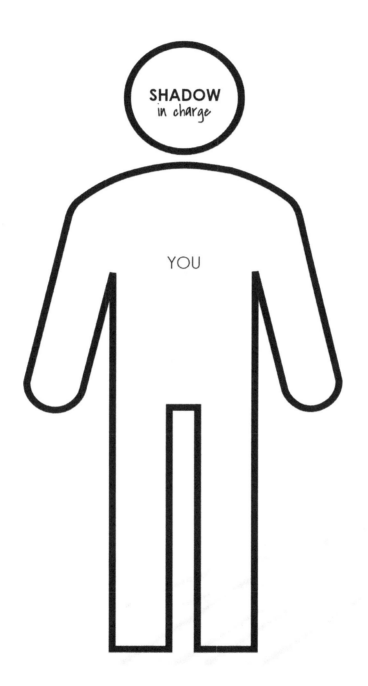

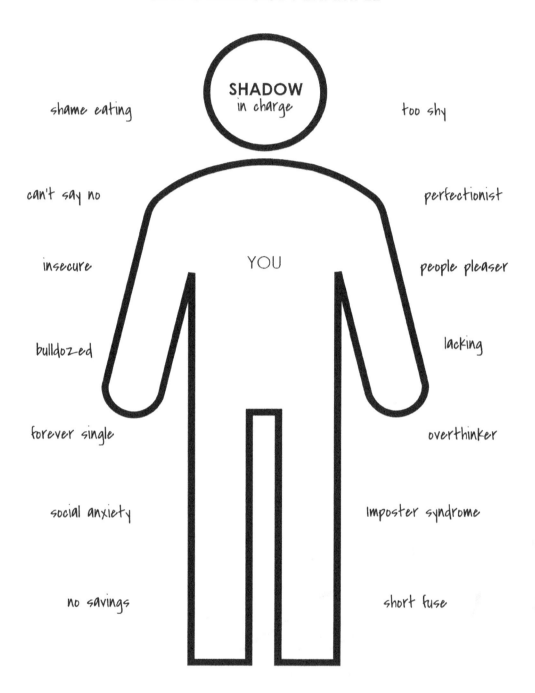

STATEMENT TO YOUR SHADOW:

SOUL in charge
(shadow is small)

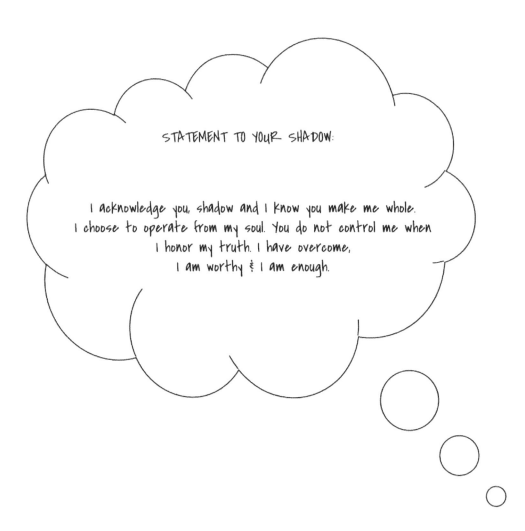

STATEMENT TO YOUR SHADOW:

I acknowledge you, shadow and I know you make me whole.
I choose to operate from my soul. You do not control me when
I honor my truth. I have overcome,
I am worthy & I am enough.

SOUL in charge
(shadow is small)

CONGRATULATIONS ON COMPLETING DAY 5

You've completed Day 5, which means you've completed the de-programming phase of your 10-day journey!

You've done amazing work in the past 5 days and have cleared years of emotional blockages, broken generational chains and have reclaimed your life – that's got to feel great.

As you move into part two, the re-programming phase of your journey, it is about putting the work you've done into action. Get ready to see significant changes in your current day-to-day and manifest the life that is meant for you.

See you tomorrow!

Ps. don't forget about the Day 5 journal page in the back of the workbook to write any additional thoughts, feelings or emotional responses that come up.

"

You've been criticizing
yourself for years and it
hasn't worked.
Try approving of
yourself and see
what happens.

- Louise Hay

"

day 6 : you vs the mirror

AFFIRM YOUR FUTURE

Congratulations on finishing part one of your Internal Intimacy journey. You have successfully completed the de-programming phase of this guide and are ready to put some of your soul-clearing work into action. These next few days consist of carefully curated exercises to help you manifest the life of your dreams - the life without attachments, societal pressure, an overbearing shadow and debilitating insecurities. The life full of truth, purpose and pure, deep love of self.

This half of your journey is all about moving forward with a clean heart and with a newfound appreciation for past experiences, lessons learned and most importantly…lessons un-learned.

Now that you have had a metaphorical cleansing, it is time to redirect your energy and take control of your limitless power. You might not realize it, but you are a force. Did you know that your heart's energetic frequency and current is so strong that it radiates 3-4 feet outside of your body? How about that what we call refer to as 'vibes' (good or bad) is actually your subconscious brain deciphering information before it can reach your conscious brain? How about the fact that your brain produces anywhere from 12-25 watts of electricity? Basically, your love can be felt from a distance, you are practically psychic and you could power a low wattage light bulb – pretty impressive.

Did you also know that the average human has approximately 60,000 thoughts a day? Here's the kicker: it is said that about 80% of them are negative, which means you can have up to 48,000 negative thoughts a day – that's a huge number! The problem with having so many negative thoughts is that your brain literally does not know the difference between what is imagined and what is real. Every far-fetched, negative, anxious and depressive thought gets catalogued and responded to in the same way that your current experience does. This oftentimes prevents you from living in the present moment and sets you up to believe that your reality is a lot more negative, anxiety-ridden and depressing than it actually is. Due to our primitive nature, having these distressing thoughts sends signals to our body that we are in the presence of immediate danger and thus, triggers a physical reaction (hence panic attacks, feeling anxious, shortness of breath, etc.). This response then leads to you to believe that something is physically wrong and circles back to the negative thinking. Do you see what just happened? One small thought about not feeling abundant or questioning your self-worth sent you into a downward spiral that left you feeling even more negative, anxious and depressed than you were five minutes ago.

The great news is, we can use the fact that our brain doesn't know the difference between thought and reality to our advantage. In the same way you tell your brain that you are having a negative experience or thought, you can just as easily tell your brain that you are having a positive experience or thought. We also know that about 95% of our thoughts are repetitive, meaning that 95% of your negative thoughts are based on what happened yesterday, last week, and even last year. Can you imagine how different your life would be if 80% of your repetitive thoughts were positive?! It's time to override negative thought patterns and start living from your soul. I can hear you saying, *it's not that easy*, and you're right, but it's also not any harder than living in constant anxiety, fear, depression and hopelessness. In order to change your life, you have to be willing to do the hard things; you have to get used to being uncomfortable and you have to know that the work you put in is worth it. It's not easy, but your future depends on it.

MIRROR MEETING

An affirmation is really anything you say out loud or think to yourself. We don't realize it, but a lot of what we are usually saying, and thinking is more negative than positive – the problem with negative words and thought patterns is that everything we say and think determines our reality. Negative thoughts equal negative experiences: our words carry a vibration that is sent out into the world and bounced back to us. Negative words emit a low vibration, which means negative energy is always being sent back to you. We must re-teach our brains to think positive thoughts about ourselves and the world around us. As said before, our brain believes what we tell it, whether real or imagined - so why not tell it that we are exactly who we want to be. Psychology Today writes, "After being studied extensively by social psychologists, self-affirmation has now just begun to receive attention. Repeated use of affirmations in a meditative state can help rewrite brain messages". By going from negative thoughts to consistent, repetitive, positive thoughts, your brain chemistry will literally change and so will your life.

I discovered the power of affirmations years ago and have never looked back…I am confident that when you see the enlightening changes in your day-to-day life, neither will you.

DAY 6 EXERCISE

STEP 1

In the left-hand column on the following page, write 5 things you feel like you struggle with daily or most often.

STEP 2

In the right-hand column, write the opposite of that struggle in the form of an 'I am' or 'I have' statement. Writing 'I am' and 'I have' statements indicates to your brain and signals to the universe that these are things that you already possess. You can also write these on a post-it note and stick them on your mirror, so they are always right in front of you.

STEP 3

Look at yourself in the mirror and say your 'I am' and 'I have' statements out loud while looking yourself in the eye. Notice how you react to each statement; if you blink, flinch, or your facial expression changes while saying your affirmations, you need say them with more conviction.

STEP 4

Repeat each statement 5X and refer back to your affirmations throughout the day when you need extra support or a reminder of your power.

If you need inspiration or want to listen to affirmations on-the-go, download either of my affirmation albums, "Everyday Affirmations" and "Everyday Love" on iTunes, Spotify or at devynpenney.com

repeat this affirmation practice for 21 consecutive days for most significant results.

THE STRUGGLE	THE AFFIRMATION

DAY 6 EXERCISE : EXAMPLE

THE STRUGGLE	THE AFFIRMATION
Feeling good about myself and my appearance.	I AM confident and I love myself exactly the way I am.
I live paycheck-to-paycheck and it stresses me out.	I AM abundant and I always have everything I need.
I hate my job but am afraid to quit.	I AM always being led on the right path; I trust that my next great opportunity is on its way to me.
I always date people who cheat on me.	I HAVE only healthy, honest & loving relationships in my life.
I have lots of anxiety, especially regarding change & fear of the unknown.	I AM safe & supported - I AM built to handle anything that comes my way.

21 DAYS TO AFFIRM YOUR FUTURE

Psychology says, it takes 21 days to form a habit.
Begin to shift your thoughts permanently from negative to positive by saying your 5X5 affirmations once a day for the next three weeks.
Cross out each day on the calendar below that you complete your affirmation practice to keep track of your progress.

day 1	day 2	day 3	day 4	day 5
day 6	day 7	day 8	day 9	day 10
day 11	day 12	day 13	day 14	day 15
day 16	day 17	day 18	day 19	day 20
day 21 you did it!				

CONGRATULATIONS ON COMPLETING DAY SIX

You're officially more than halfway through this guide! I'm hoping that you are beginning to settle into your soul-level self and are beginning to believe that your dream life is both possible and attainable.

Keep pushing, I see you.

See you tomorrow!

Ps. don't forget about the Day 6 journal page in the back of the workbook to write any additional thoughts, feelings or emotional responses that come up

"

You must attach yourself spiritually to what you have placed in your imagination as a future fact, and never allow anyone, anything, any circumstance, no matter how persuasive their case, to alter what you know to be your destiny.

- Wayne Dyer

"

day 7 : you & your future

BELIEVE IT TO SEE IT

Now that you are reminded of just how powerful your brain is and realize the kind of influence that your thoughts have over your future, let's talk about manifestation. As self-help books and law of attraction conversations have become more popular over the last few years, it seems like everyone is talking about manifesting the future, but what does that actually *mean?*

Truthfully, you've been manifesting your life since the time you were young. If our thoughts and words create our reality, everything that you have said and thought up until this point has shaped your world.

The Law of Attraction states, "Simply put, the Law of Attraction is the ability to attract into our lives whatever we are focusing on. It is believed that regardless of age, nationality or religious belief, we are all susceptible to the laws which govern the Universe, including the Law of Attraction. It is the Law of Attraction which uses the power of the mind to translate whatever is in our thoughts and materialize them into reality. In basic terms, all thoughts turn into things eventually".

Whether you realize it or not, you quite literally have the ability to speak and think things into existence. Look at your life…is it everything that you want it to be? If your answer is, *no*, what negative thoughts and words are you willing to give up in order for your world to reflect your innermost truth and desires?

You've done amazing work clearing old beliefs and breaking out of social constructs. Now, it is time to take your future into your own hands. You are no longer held down by the weight of other people's opinions, nor are you held back by your shadow. Everything that you want for yourself is available to you and nothing that is meant for you will pass you by. It's time to begin actively manifesting the life that is meant for you.

DAY 6 EXERCISE : VISION BOARD

The extremely cool thing about manifestation is that everything that you can imagine in your head is placed there, uniquely for you. Think about it this way; when you daydream, think about your five-year plan, etc. you see specific snapshots of things you want and are maybe even able to place yourself in the frame, right? That vision is yours and only yours – your co-worker doesn't have the same dream, your sibling can't visualize what you can, your best friend's dream life looks different than yours does. The frustration in this is that other people can't see what you can, which is why many will project their own visions for themselves (or lack thereof) onto you. On the flip side, your brain has created a vision that only you have, which means that it is attainable. Your ability to visualize, imagine and create futuristic snapshots in your head is a gift; use it!

STEP 1

If you want to create a physical vision board, use the following piece of paper or a separate paper or canvas.

If you want to create a virtual vision board, use whichever computer program (I recommend PowerPoint for ease) or phone app (I recommend CollageMaker).

STEP 2

Refer back to your day 1 meditation journal and look over the descriptions you used to describe your highest self/life. Take note of the things you felt, what you saw, what you smelled, who you were with, etc.

STEP 3

Begin gathering images and quotes – either from magazines, social media, google images, etc. – that tangibly reflect those dreams, visions, feelings and future aspirations.

some image ideas:

- home décor inspiration
- nature/travel
- 'power couples'/ideal relationship inspiration
- health/fitness/wellness/nutrition
- inspirational/motivational quotes
- anything else that you dream of – this is for you!

STEP 4

Make a collage of content and materials which allow you to see your future in front of you. Refer to this visual manifestation often and believe that because you can see it, it is meant for you. Don't restrict yourself with timelines and 'rules', just allow yourself to bask in your desires. You can update your vision board or create multiple, as your dreams become reality.

Some of my clients go as far as to take pictures or screenshots of their boards and use them as their phone/computer/tablet backgrounds to accelerate manifestation. If it is constantly top of mind, you are more apt to seek it out and draw it in.

There is no right or wrong way to create – have fun with it; turn up some music, color outside the lines, enjoy yourself and start manifesting your awesome future!

CONGRATULATIONS ON COMPLETING DAY SEVEN

Day 7 is one of my favorite days because it allows you to think about your future - giving you an opportunity to flex your creative muscle and to get out of your own head a bit.

You're getting so close to completing this 10-day journey and I'm so proud that you've made it this far.

Don't forget to do your affirmations (if you haven't already) and I can't wait to see you tomorrow – you're kicking ass!

Ps. don't forget about the Day 7 journal page in the back of the workbook to write any additional thoughts, feelings or emotional responses that come up.

"

It takes mental discipline
to align with who you
really are.

- Abraham

"

day 8: you by discipline

PATH TO SUCCESS

All this talk of affirmations, visualization and manifestation should have you feeling excited about your future and what you now know is possible for you. While the work you've put into the exercises thus far has been amazing, actualizing your goals takes a certain level of mental discipline and we've only just scratched the surface.

So far, you've cleared energetic blockages, dismissed societal burdens and have looked yourself in the eye to see your soul for exactly who you are. Hopefully, you feel like a major pressure has been lifted and that a newfound freedom has taken the place of endless stress and shame. Now, it is time to talk about the day-to-day routine that will help move you forward and show you tangible progress as your journey continues.

Today is also the day the you will reach a fork in the road and will have to choose between two paths. The path on the right-hand side leads you on a long, winding road to ultimate freedom, soul-level living and a multitude of successes . The path on the left-hand side will lead you on a short, straight path back to a life that is unenjoyable, but comfortable. Which path would you like to take?

80% of you are staring at the page and without hesitation want to take the path to success.

10% of you need a minute to think about it.

10% of you are leaning toward the path back to comfort.

100% of you are ready to walk the path on the right.

50% of you actually will.

Here's why: as humans, we are more afraid of success than we are of failure. Our society has normalized failure so much that we aren't phased by it, in fact, we expect it. Success on the other hand, is more foreign to us. We are made to believe that success is linear: it is exclusively for the 'taking' and can only be achieved by 'hustling' 24/7, sacrificing everything that brings you joy and becoming a slave to the almighty dollar. We are afraid to succeed; not because we can't, but because we believe we can't. We fear achievement because we don't know ourselves well enough to know if we can *maintain* it. What happens if we do everything we are supposed to, we make it to the top and then it all comes crashing down? What if we get a taste of success and then we lose it? What if we dream big and are crushed by our reality?

These are valid questions and concerns – success, in whatever capacity, takes work. Think about weight loss for example, anyone can lose weight, but only a select few can actually keep that weight off…not because it is impossible, but because it takes a level of discipline that most are not willing to endure. For that reason, many people won't even try to lose weight because they don't want to be disappointed when they gain it back. Do you see what we do to ourselves? Fear is a constant soundtrack playing in the background and it's just loud enough to stop us from moving forward. Fear tells us that comfortable is safe, even if it's also lackluster, unsatisfying and even, miserable. Here's the great news: we are built for disappointment. The reason that failure has become so normalized is because so many people have experienced it and survived it…every time.

I'm encouraging you to take the path to success because I know you can do it and you will, if you give yourself the opportunity. You don't need to know exactly how, you don't need to fear disappointment, or to worry about the *what if.* All you have to do is live in the *what is*, take small steps forward every day and know that you have in your soul what it takes to succeed on every level.

Jump and build the plane on the way down.

DAY 8 EXERCISE : YOUR DAILY 7

We allow fear to paralyze us because we lack confidence. We don't believe we can achieve the big dreams, we don't know who we are when we are operating at 100%, we don't even trust that we can figure things out along the way. We wait for perfection to act – the perfect moment, the perfect idea, the perfect circumstance. The only problem with that is that *perfect* doesn't exist. Knowing that, you have two options: wait forever or build the self confidence you need in order to *just go for it*. I'm going to go with the latter.

The purpose of this exercise is to identify small, daily practices that make a large difference in the big picture. The easiest and most effective way to build confidence within yourself is to build trust by keeping promises to yourself. The more you do what you say you will, the more you believe in your ability to do what you think you can. Start treating yourself as your own best friend; if you told someone you loved that you would pick them up from the airport, would you just not show up? If not, why is it then okay to tell yourself that you are going to do something and then not honor your commitment? Are you not as important as your friend is? It's time to start keeping your word to yourself and to others. Look inward, listen to what your mind, body and soul need and then feed your needs. Respect yourself enough to be disciplined in your process. You can do this; all you have to do is commit!

STEP 1

In the space provided, brainstorm six things that you need on a daily basis in order to have a successful day. Make these practices small, for example: drink 8 glasses of water, make your bed, stretch, read for 20 minutes…I've added your daily affirmations as the 7th, so that is already included.

STEP 2

Write each of these practices down, in no particular order and tweak them until you have what you believe is the perfect Daily 7. These will be different for everyone and while most will be wellness-based, you have to be honest with yourself about your needs. If you need a nightly glass of wine to wind down and that is what makes a successful day for you, then add that to your Daily 7. There is no shame in this game, this is about doing what makes you feel good and what is truly best for you.

STEP 3

Aim to incorporate all 7 practices into your everyday life – warning: if you *do* maintain these daily practices, I guarantee you will begin reaching your goals in no time.

STEP 4

When you don't reach all 7 practices, don't beat yourself up! Even incorporating one practice a day is a huge win and a big step in the right direction. You got 2 out of the 7 in today? Amazing! Again, this is about setting yourself up for success based on whatever makes you feel good. If tomorrow you drink 6 glasses of water instead of 8, acknowledge your accomplishment and move on. The point of doing the Daily 7 is to build up trust and confidence by keeping small promises to yourself. Doing all 7 will make a tangible difference, doing 1 is still keeping a promise to yourself – that's not failure, that's building a lifestyle.

STEP 5

Use these Daily 7 as a guide for your day-to-day routine; if you practice daily, you will see a noticeable difference in your life. Feeling overwhelmed, tired, anxious, stressed or just *off*? Refer back your list, choose one or two of your Daily 7 and get back on your path to success.

YOUR DAILY 7

7 small steps that make a huge difference

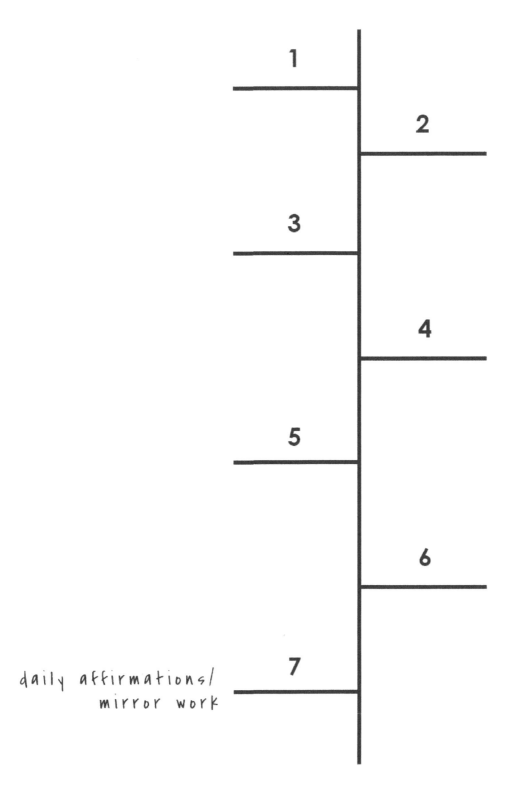

1

2

3

4

5

6

7

daily affirmations/
mirror work

YOUR DAILY 7

7 small steps that make a huge difference

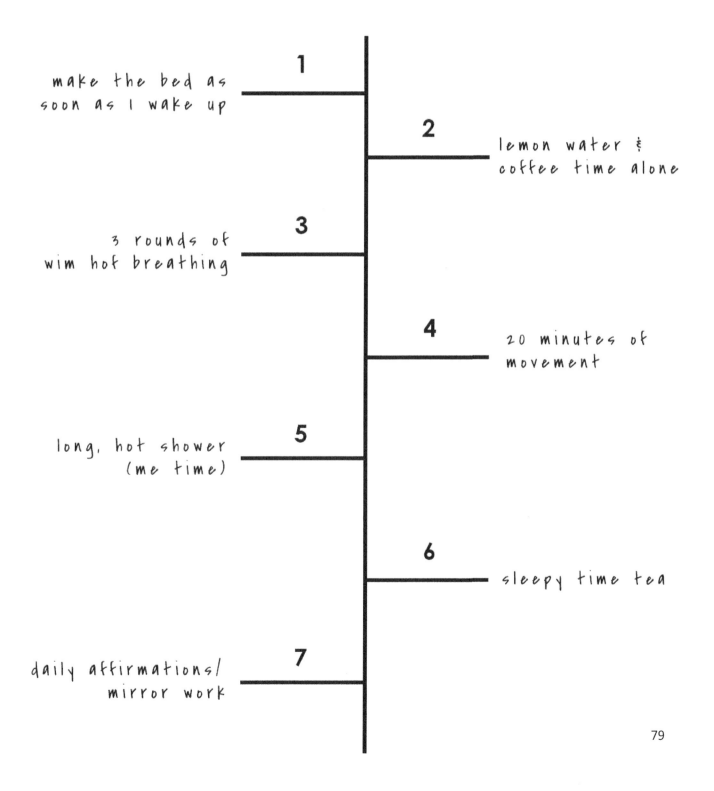

1 make the bed as soon as I wake up

2 lemon water & coffee time alone

3 3 rounds of wim hof breathing

4 20 minutes of movement

5 long, hot shower (me time)

6 sleepy time tea

7 daily affirmations/ mirror work

CONGRATULATIONS ON COMPLETING DAY EIGHT

If you're reading this, it means you've chosen the path to success. Awesome!

You're so close to having completed your 10-day journey, I'm so excited for you and know that you will take the exercises from the last three days and be able to use them to your advantage for the rest of your life.

Don't forget to do your affirmations (if you haven't already) – I'll see you tomorrow for your final clearing exercise – get psyched!

I'm proud of you.

Ps. don't forget about the Day 8 journal page in the back of the workbook to write any additional thoughts, feelings or emotional responses that come up.

"

The practice of
forgiveness is our most
important contribution to
the healing of the world.
- Marianne Williamson

"

day 9 : you vs. forgiveness

CLEAR YOUR HEART

You have come so far in just 9 days:

You have successfully cleared many emotional roadblocks; you have rid yourself of a great deal of guilt and shame and you have realized that no one knows you better than you know yourself. You have created a clear vision of your future and have begun to work towards it every day, because you know you are worth the time, energy and investment. Most importantly, you have realized that when you live from the inside out, you are fucking unstoppable!

It feels so good to tell you that you are one day away from *Mastering the Art of Internal Intimacy* – I am extremely proud of your journey thus far and know that it will extend far past these 10 days.

That said, today is about taking the final step in this process – forgiving yourself and others. We cannot fully move forward until your heart, head and soul are completely free of any and all resentment. We have moved through the past 9 days quickly, which means that some lingering feelings of disappointment, anger and bitterness have probably been swept under the rug. Today, we're lifting the rug up and sweeping those crumbs of resentment up for good.

It is difficult to compartmentalize your past, present and future – which is why feelings of anxiety and depression are so common. In order to move forward however, it is your duty to face your feelings and heal them. As we have moved through the last 8 exercises, we have focused on uncovering realities that you maybe weren't aware of and it is natural to feel like at some points you have been lied to, deceived and failed by your direct influences, society and even yourself. It is our nature as humans to deflect responsibility, so that it is not our fault when we fail or when we aren't where we want to be mentally, physically and emotionally.

What we have trouble understanding in the moment, and sometimes long after, is that every person, every situation, every emotion, every moment is meant for us. I don't believe that everything 'happens for a reason', but I do believe that everything has meaning. If we can find that meaning, we are able to adopt gratitude rather than blame. It is easier to blame people for what they have, or haven't, done *to* you rather than think of what they have done *for* you. Yet, our power lies in the lessons we have learned along the way. Every single thing has led you to this moment, right here, right now. If that isn't something to be grateful for, I don't know what is.

DAY 9 EXERCISE: RELEASE RESENTMENT

The purpose of this exercise is not only to forgive, but to also employ empathy and give thanks to those who have shown you the light. Gratitude for every experience, negative or positive, is the only way to fully release any and all negativity. It is time to take full responsibility for your life; no one has the ability to influence you unless you allow them to. Relish in the lessons you've learned and get excited about the endless possibilities that lie ahead in your future as a free thinker.

STEP 1

Forgive yourself.

The disappointment we have in ourselves for not 'doing making changes sooner', 'relying too much on others', 'looking for outside validation', 'doing what we're told', etc. can easily overpower the process of healing. Feel it all and then let go – your future literally depends on it.

see Day 9 'self' exercise and fill in the blanks to complete

STEP 2

Forgive others.

It is easy to feel like we have been led astray and failed by the people who we think 'love us the most'. This sends us into an endless spiral of questioning that leads to resentment and eventually, hatred. That is so *low vibe*. Understand that everyone is doing the best they can with the exact tools they have in that moment. What is best for others is not always best for you and what is best for you is not always best for others. Neither is good or bad or right or wrong, it just is. Have empathy for people who are different than you, forgive and move on.

see Day 9 'direct influence' exercise and fill in the blanks to complete

STEP 3

Forgive the external world.

Up until now, you have allowed yourself to be swayed by external circumstances because you believed that the outside world knew you better than you knew yourself. Now, you realize that no one knows you like your soul does. Your work is internal; society doesn't matter, social media doesn't matter…you, honoring your truth matters. You've already spent too much time thinking about what goes on outside of you. It's time to fully live from the inside out – forgive so you can do that.

see Day 9 'society' exercise and fill in the blanks to complete

SELF

I forgive _____,

for making me feel

_____

_____.

I now know that

_____

and I choose to _____.

I thank myself for

_____.

_____,

… I clear my heart, my head & my soul of

_____.

DAY 9 EXERCISE : EXAMPLE

SELF

I forgive MYSELF ,

for making me feel

I didn't have enough power to enjoy the life that I want for myself

and for self-sabotaging for years because I didn't believe in myself .

I now know that

I have been programmed for my entire life ,

and I choose to de-program and begin honoring my soul .

I thank myself for

taking responsibility for myself and taking action by starting this ,

process 9 days ago and sticking with it .

… I clear my heart, my head & my soul of

all guilt, self-doubt and any fear of moving forward .

DIRECT INFLUENCES

I forgive _____,

for making me feel

_____

_____.

I now know that

_____,

and I choose to _____.

I thank myself for

_____.

_____,

… I clear my heart, my head & my soul of

_____.

DIRECT INFLUENCES

I forgive MY PARENTS ,

for making me feel
like I had to do things their way and like there was only one, very

traditional path available to me + prioritizing money over happiness .

I now know that
they did the best they could with their programming and tools ,

and I choose to break those generational chains .

I thank them for
wanting what they believe is best for me and for making opportunities,
available to me that I wouldn't have had otherwise. .

… I clear my heart, my head & my soul of
any resentment towards them .

SOCIETY

I forgive _____,

for making me feel

_____

_____.

I now know that

_____,

and I choose to _____.

I thank myself for

_____.

_____,

… I clear my heart, my head & my soul of

_____.

SOCIETY

I forgive SOCIETY, SOCIAL MEDIA & CELEBRITIES ,

for making me feel
like I am not good enough; like I always have to be in better shape,

make more money, be better looking & strive for perfection .

I now know that
I am enough. ,

and I choose to run my own race, without outside influence .

I thank them for
showing me that no matter how fit, wealthy or 'perfect' I am, ,
none of it matters unless I'm living for myself and from my soul .

… I clear my heart, my head & my soul of
anger, jealousy and feelings of inadequacy .

CONGRATULATIONS ON COMPLETING DAY NINE

I hope you're feeling lighter after completing that exercise. Forgiveness allows us to let go of emotions we have been subconsciously holding onto for years. It feels amazing to finally release. You are almost there.

See you tomorrow for our final day together, cheers to you and all of your hard work!

Ps. don't forget about the Day 9 journal page in the back of the workbook to write any additional thoughts, feelings or emotional responses that come up.

"

...and you scare people because you are whole all by yourself.

- Lauren Alex Hooper

"

CONGRATULATIONS

You did it! 10 days of extensive, emotional, amazing work – I am so proud of you.

While I know that this is just the beginning of your soul journey, I hope that this guide has acted as a catalyst in wanting to get to know yourself better, love yourself deeper and live the life that is available to you.

The only time I believe in reminiscing about the past is to acknowledge how far you've come, so let's recap the last 10 days, shall we?

DAY 1

You met your highest self, saw glimpses of your future and harnessed your inner power and calm.

DAY 2

You recognized your conditioning and cancelled old belief systems that no longer serve you.

DAY 3

You let go of the standards of perfection you've been holding yourself to according to 'society'.

DAY 4

You faced guilt, shame and insecurity head on and turned your negative responses into your power.

DAY 5

You acknowledged your shadow and made peace with it by learning to shine your light even brighter.

DAY 6

You looked yourself in the eye and told your brain who you really are.

DAY 7

You began to actively manifest your future by visualizing all that you now know is possible.

DAY 8

You created a structure that will help you keep promises to yourself, building trust and confidence.

DAY 9

You cleared your heart fully and let go of resentment and negativity that has been weighing you down.

WOW!

You are impressive; look at how much you have accomplished, purely because you committed to yourself and the process.

If this 10-day journey has taught you anything, it is that you are extremely powerful. Your mind, body and soul got you here, even when it was hard. You pushed past your limits, you stepped out of your comfort zone, you did it afraid, alone and unsure. You continued to show up every day for yourself. You surrendered to the process and you have made progress as a result.

As said, I know that this is just the beginning for you; I know that you will go on to be an even better version of your soul self. You will continue to de-program and un-learn. You will stumble along the way, but you will keep going, because that is who you are.

You have proven to yourself that you *are* the warrior, the truth-teller, the badass, the empath, the soul-searcher, the peacekeeper, the disruptor, the rockstar, the creator, the lover, the intuitive, the rebel, the eternal optimist.

You are limitless.

DAY 10 EXERCISE: REVISIT DAY

When you first met your highest self and visualized your future, you hadn't yet acknowledged your conditioning or begun the de-programming process.

Now that you have done such an inspiring job of clearing old beliefs, negative thoughts and listening to your soul, I'd like you to revisit your highest self. I want you to do the same mediation and journaling exercise that you did on Day 1 while paying attention to your current mindset and newfound freedom of thought. I believe that since you are much clearer and lighter after 10 days of extensive work, you will be able to see more, feel more and dream even bigger.

As you move beyond this 10-day process, it is important to continue to allow your vision of your highest self and most purposeful life to expand. Continue to clear, continue to question, continue to become more aware of yourself and your surroundings. Continue to think big…no, bigger. Continue to listen to your soul, continue to surrender to the support, protection and guidance that is available to you. Continue to love. Continue to return to yourself.

HIGHEST SELF (SOUL) MEETING MEDITATION & MANIFESTATION (20-25 MINUTES)

Silence and visualization are two of the greatest tools you have when getting to know yourself. Sitting still with your own thoughts allows your subconscious to reveal itself and visualization allows your soul desires to surface.

SILENCE /MEDITATION
For many people, meditation is intimidating, which is understandable because sitting with your own thoughts can be intimidating – you're never sure what's going to come up.
That said, you cannot let go of what you do not realize you're holding onto.

The key is to shift your perspective from being afraid of being alone with yourself to being grateful for the opportunity to work through thoughts and feelings that have been weighing you down.

The more you allow yourself to feel, the easier it is to let go of the negativity and make way for your highest self to show up.

VISUALIZATION /MANIFESTATION

Manifestation is the light amidst the darkness. The cool thing about your mind is that it won't allow you to visualize anything that isn't possible or attainable. Every daydream and vision that you have regarding your perfect life exists in real time and is waiting for you to claim what is yours. Having a clear vision of your future is what keeps you going during even the most difficult times. Knowing who you are capable of existing as and being able to see your own potential is one of life's greatest gifts.

Combining these two practices is extremely powerful and is the perfect way to begin your journey.

I've created this custom, guided meditation in order to help you 'meet' your highest self.

The following recording is meant to be consumed while sitting or laying down in a comfortable, quiet place and will take approximately 15 minutes to run through (you can do it!).

Immediately following your meditation experience, please take another 5-10 minutes to record details of your highest self as you saw him/her in your meditation, be as specific as possible.

CONGRATULATIONS ON COMPLETING,
"MASTERING THE ART OF INTERNAL ITIMACY"

I'm proud of you, I believe in you, I am excited for you and I love you.
Congratulations doesn't even cover it - keep moving forward, you deserve it.
Ps. don't forget about the Day 10 journal page in the back of the workbook to write any additional thoughts, feelings or emotional responses that come up.

I'm here for you now and always:

never hesitate to reach out & connect:
email: devyn@devynpenney.com

for more information or to book a one-on-one session, visit:
www.devynpenney.com

love, Dev

day 1 journal

OVERALL, I FEEL:

_____

_____

_____

_____

_____

_____

_____

_____

_____

_____

_____

_____

_____

_____

_____

_____

day 2 journal

OVERALL, I FEEL:

day 3 journal

OVERALL, I FEEL:

_____

_____

_____

_____

_____

_____

_____

_____

_____

_____

_____

_____

_____

_____

day 4 journal

OVERALL, I FEEL:

_____

_____

_____

_____

_____

_____

_____

_____

_____

_____

_____

_____

_____

_____

_____

_____

day 5 journal

OVERALL, I FEEL:

_____

_____

_____

_____

_____

_____

_____

_____

_____

_____

_____

_____

_____

_____

_____

OVERALL, I FEEL:

day 7 journal

OVERALL, I FEEL:

_____

_____

_____

_____

_____

_____

_____

_____

_____

_____

_____

_____

_____

_____

_____

day 8 journal

OVERALL, I FEEL:

_____

_____

_____

_____

_____

_____

_____

_____

_____

_____

_____

_____

_____

_____

day 9 journal

OVERALL, I FEEL:

_____

_____

_____

_____

_____

_____

_____

_____

_____

_____

_____

_____

_____

_____

_____

day 10 journal

OVERALL, I FEEL:

_____

_____

_____

_____

_____

_____

_____

_____

_____

_____

_____

_____

_____

_____

_____

_____

SOUL-LEVEL SELF CARE

the first three words/phrases you see are
what you need most of today

```
K H I A D K S E A T C L E A N L D D C N
T Y W B F R Z G R A T I T U D E L I S T
A D M O V E M E N T Z I A V X M R P H J
K R P X V A P O W E R S O N G O O M W S
E A H B U D P O J H V D O G Q N U Q S A
A T O R L A D R O R X W C E P W T M T Y
B E N E E N A G U K X I V V S A I T R N
A P E A S O M A R M W G F D Y T N N E O
T V A T S S E N N K M R H X L E E Z T O
H C F H E O D I A Y P E R F J R M K C G
Q A R I N C I Z L D E E P B R E A T H R
Y N I N T I T E P L R Z E Q P P D X O D
S C E G I A A M X N O A L C O H O L K F
I E N S A L T H O T S H O W E R I P I G
L L D W L M E Y A F F I R M A T I O N S
E P R E O E N V K I W D T A K E A N A P
N L Q A I D D A I L Y S E V E N H B B W
C A Y T L I A I R P L A N E M O D E H A
E N Y U S A Z I V A S Z F H X Z M U J L
X S J L M A K E Y O U R B E D V R C G K
```

SOUL-LEVEL SELF CARE

the first three words/phrases you see are what you need most of today

```
K  H  I  A  D  K  S  E  A  T  C  L  E  A  N  L  D  D  C  N
T  Y  W  B  F  R  Z  G  R  A  T  I  T  U  D  E  L  I  S  T
A  D  M  O  V  E  M  E  N  T  Z  I  A  V  X  M  R  P  H  J
K  R  P  X  V  A  P  O  W  E  R  S  O  N  G  O  O  M  W  S
E  A  H  B  U  D  P  O  J  H  V  D  O  G  Q  N  U  Q  S  A
A  T  O  R  L  A  D  R  O  R  X  W  C  E  P  W  T  M  T  Y
B  E  N  E  A  D  R  O  U  K  X  I  V  V  S  A  I  M  R  N
A  P  E  A  S  R  G  U  R  M  W  G  F  D  Y  T  N  N  E  O
T  V  A  T  S  N  A  R  N  K  M  R  H  X  L  E  E  Z  T  O
H  C  F  H  E  O  M  N  A  Y  P  E  R  F  J  R  M  K  C  G
Q  A  R  I  N  S  E  A  I  D  E  E  P  B  R  E  A  T  H  R
Y  N  I  N  T  O  D  I  Z  L  R  Z  E  Q  P  P  D  X  O  D
S  C  E  G  I  C  I  T  E  P  L  R  Z  E  Q  P  P  D  X  O
I  E  N  S  A  I  T  A  M  X  N  O  A  L  C  O  H  O  L  K  F
L  L  D  W  L  A  A  M  T  H  O  T  S  H  O  W  E  R  I  P  I  G
E  P  R  E  M  L  M  E  Y  A  F  F  I  R  M  A  T  I  O  N  S
N  L  Q  A  E  O  E  N  V  K  I  W  D  T  A  K  E  A  N  A  P
C  A  N  T  I  I  D  D  A  I  L  Y  S  E  V  E  N  H  B  B  W
E  N  Y  U  L  L  I  A  I  R  P  L  A  N  E  M  O  D  E  H  A
X  S  J  L  M  A  K  E  Y  O  U  R  B  E  D  V  R  C  G  K
```

Found words/phrases: EAT CLEAN, GRATITUDE LIST, MOVEMENT, POWER SONG, DEEP BREATH, NO ALCOHOL, HOT SHOWER, AFFIRMATIONS, TAKE A NAP, DAILY SEVEN, AIRPLANE MODE, MAKE YOUR BED, TAKE A BATH, HYDRATE, PHONE A FRIEND, CANCEL PLANS, SILENCE, SAY NO, STRETCH, ROUTINE, JOURNAL, ORGANIZE, MEDITATE, ESSENTIAL OILS, SWEAT, WALK

about the author

Devyn Penney is an international life coach specializing in intimacy. She has worked with coaching clients all over the world, helping them get to know themselves better, love themselves more and empower them to live lives full of purpose and peace.

A born entrepreneur and thought leader, Devyn has spent her career helping people feel confident and unafraid to express themselves fully.

When she's not on a coaching call or creating content, Devyn enjoys weekly SoulCycle classes, reading the latest self-development best seller and a perfectly made skinny margarita.

Currently residing in New York, you can oftentimes find Devyn walking through the city with headphones in, aviators on and a large, dark roast coffee in hand.

For more information on Devyn or to book a one-on-one coaching session, please visit : www.devynpenney.com.

"

my mission is, and has always been, to increase the amount of love in the world by showing people how to love themselves.

- Devyn Penney

"

acknowledgements

I want to take a moment to thank the people who have always supported my own journey and have allowed me to be my soul-level self, despite all of the ups, downs and re-programming.

To my parents, Mindy & Bob and my siblings, Ashton, Bobby & Spencer - thank you for being the most solid foundation of love.

To my life coach and first phone call, Daune – thank you for always believing in me and pushing me to be my highest self.

To my cousin, Jess – thank you for talking me through all of my best (and worst) moments and making me laugh along the way.

To my day ones, you know who you are – thank you for cheering me on every day.

To all of you, who make me show up every day as the best version of myself. Thank you for your endless love and support in everything I do.

I love and appreciate you all more than I could ever fully express.

Thank you for talking me through writing a self-development book during a quarantine, a global pandemic and a revolution – you've all contributed more than you know.

notes

Brown, B. (2013). *Daring Greatly: How the Courage to Be Vulnerable Transforms the Way We Live, Love, Parent, and Lead*. Penguin UK.

DK. (2015). *The Psychology Book*. Penguin.

Dunne, C. (2015). *Carl Jung: Wounded Healer of the Soul*. Watkins Media Limited.

Hay, L. L. (2003). *You Can Heal Your Life*.

Jung, C. (2016). *Psychological Types*. Routledge.

Speaks, T. A. (n.d.). Psychology Today: Health, Help, Happiness + Find a Therapist.

(n.d.). The Law Of Attraction - Discover How to Improve Your Life.

Made in the USA
Middletown, DE
23 December 2020